This book is the perfect way to add delicious pizza recipes to your family's menu. With a wide selection of delicious and tasty pizzas, everyone will be sure to find something they love. From classic pepperoni pizzas to creative new topping combinations, this cookbook has something for every pizza lover in your household. All the recipes are easy-to-follow and can be made with commonly available ingredients, so you won't have to go out of your way to enjoy delicious homemade pizza. Enjoy the delicious taste of freshly-baked pizza anytime with these delicious recipes!

How To Make A Pizza Dough

If you love delicious pizza, then learning how to make your own dough is essential. Here's a quick guide to get you started on your delicious pizza-making journey.

To begin, gather the ingredients needed for pizza dough: all-purpose flour, yeast, warm water, salt and olive oil. Measure out one and a half cups of flour into a large mixing bowl and add two teaspoons of active dry yeast. Pour in three-quarters cup of warm water and whisk until smooth. Stir in one teaspoon of salt and two tablespoons of olive oil before kneading the dough with your hands until it forms a ball. Alternatively, use an electric mixer with a dough hook attachment or food processor to mix the ingredients together.

Once the dough is mixed and kneaded, cover the bowl with plastic wrap and let it rise for about an hour. After that, your delicious pizza dough is ready to use for all sorts of delicious pizza recipes! To shape your pizzas, lightly flour a surface and roll out the dough until you reach the desired size and shape. Top with delicious toppings of your choice, then bake in a preheated oven at 425°F for 15-20 minutes or until golden brown. Enjoy your delicious homemade pizza!

Now that you have mastered how to make delicious pizza dough, you can get creative with different recipes and toppings – giving you endless possibilities when it comes to delicious homemade pizzas. Get started today on your delicious pizza-making journey!

Guidelines:

1. Always make sure to use the correct measurements of ingredients when making pizza dough. This will ensure your delicious homemade pizzas turn out perfect every time.
2. When rolling out your dough, lightly flour a surface and roll until you reach the desired size and shape.
3. Preheat oven to 425°F before baking, then bake for 15-20 minutes or until golden brown.
4. Allow the dough to rise for about an hour before forming into a ball for baking – this allows for delicious flavor development in your pizza crusts!
5. Get creative with different delicious recipes and toppings – giving you endless possibilities when it comes to delicious homemade pizzas.
6. Enjoy your delicious homemade pizza!

Follow these simple steps and you will be making delicious, homemade pizzas in no time! With a little practice, you'll be an expert pizza maker – enjoying delicious recipes with friends and family in no time. Bon appétit!

Margherita Pizza

Margherita pizza is one of the most delicious and classic pizzas that you can prepare at home. It's a simple recipe, but when done right, it has an incredible flavor. To make a Margherita pizza, you'll need a 112-inch round of pizza dough that's been stretched out nicely; 3 tablespoons tomato sauce; extra-virgin olive oil; 2¾ ounces fresh mozzarella; and 4 to 5 basil leaves, roughly torn.

Begin by preheating your oven to 500°F. Place the stretched-out pizza dough on a lightly oiled parchment paper-lined baking sheet or directly onto your preheated baking stone. Spread the tomato sauce evenly onto the crust followed by a drizzle of olive oil.

Next, add the mozzarella cheese and arrange the torn basil leaves atop. Place your pizza in the oven and bake for 8 to 10 minutes or until golden brown. Serve warm and enjoy!

This delicious Margherita pizza can easily be made at home with a few simple ingredients. Follow these steps and you'll have a delicious, classic Italian-style pizza right at your fingertips! Experience delicious Italian flavors today with this delicious Margherita pizza recipe. Enjoy!

Cheese Pizza

Are you craving delicious pizza but don't know how to prepare one? Look no further, as we have the perfect cheese pizza recipe for you! To make this delicious meal, you will need 1/2 recipe of homemade pizza crust, 1/2-3/4 cup (127-190g) of your favorite pizza sauce (homemade or store-bought), 8 ounces of sliced mozzarella cheese, 1 and 1/2 cups (6oz or 168g) shredded mozzarella cheese, 2-3 Tablespoons (10-15g) grated Parmesan cheese, and dried basil or Italian seasoning.

To begin, preheat your oven to 425°F (218°C). Then spread out the pizza dough on a baking sheet or pizza pan. Next, spread the sauce over the pizza crust, then top with sliced and shredded mozzarella cheese. Sprinkle parmesan cheese and dried basil/Italian seasoning over the top of the pizza. Bake for 12-15 minutes until the cheese is melted and golden brown. Let cool slightly before cutting into slices to serve. Enjoy your delicious homemade cheese pizza!

With a few simple ingredients, you can enjoy delicious homemade cheese pizza in no time! So what are you waiting for? Try out this delicious recipe today!

Taco Pizza

NGREDIENTS

1 (12-16 OUNCE) PIZZA DOUGH, (DEPENDING ON IF YOU
WANT THICK OR THIN CRUST)
1 LB GROUND BEEF.
1 (1 OUNCE) PACKET OF TACO SEASONING.
1 (15 OUNCE) CAN REFRIED BEANS.
1/4 CUP SALSA.
2 CUPS SHREDDED CHEDDAR CHEESE , (OR MEXICAN BLEND
CHEESE)
SLICED OLIVES, (ABOUT 1/4 CUP)

Taco pizza is a delicious and easy meal to prepare. Start by preheating your oven to 375°F (190°C). To make the dough, roll out the pizza dough and place it onto a lightly greased baking sheet.

Next, cook the ground beef in a skillet over medium heat until browned. Once done, stir in the taco seasoning until combined. Spread the refried beans over the pizza crust, followed by the cooked ground beef. Top with salsa and cheese of your choice (cheddar or Mexican blend). Finally, top with sliced olives before baking for 20-25 minutes or until golden brown.

Once done, remove from oven and let cool for 5-10 minutes. Slice into pieces and enjoy your delicious taco pizza. With a few simple ingredients, you can create a delicious and savory meal in no time! Try out other delicious pizza recipes to satisfy your craving for something delicious. Bon Appetit!

Arugula Pizza

INGREDIENTS

1 ¼ cup pizza sauce (purchased or our favorite
Easy Pizza Sauce)
1 cup (3 ounces) shredded smoked gouda
cheese.
½ cup shredded Parmesan cheese.
6 ounces fresh mozzarella cheese.
4 cups (3 ounces) baby arugula.
1 tablespoon extra virgin olive oil.
¼ teaspoon kosher salt, plus more for
sprinkling.

If you're looking for delicious pizza recipes, look no further than this delicious arugula pizza. This delicious and easy-to-prepare meal is perfect for any day of the week. To make it, start by preheating your oven to 500°F (260°C). Next, spread 1 ¼ cups of purchased or homemade pizza sauce on a 12 inch baking sheet lined with parchment paper. Top with 1 cup (3 ounces) shredded smoked gouda cheese, ½ cup shredded Parmesan cheese, and 6 ounces fresh mozzarella cheese. Bake in the preheated oven for 10 minutes until golden brown and bubbly. Once done baking, top the pizza with 4 cups (3 ounces) baby arugula and sprinkle with 1 tablespoon extra virgin olive oil and ¼ teaspoon kosher salt. Slice, serve, and enjoy! With its delicious combination of flavors, this delicious arugula pizza is sure to become a family favorite. Enjoy!

Spinach Alfredo Pizza

Ingredients

1 13 oz puff pastry sheet.
½ cup Alfredo sauce any jar or type will work.
12 oz. marinated artichoke hearts chopped.
1 cup fresh spinach leaves.
2 Tbsp. green onions chopped.
8 oz. log mozzarella cheese sliced.
½ cup parmesan cheese shredded.
1 Tbsp. Everything Bagel seasoning ad.!

This delicious Spinach Alfredo Pizza is a great way to enjoy a delicious pizza without having to order from your favorite pizzeria. With its delicious combination of Alfredo sauce, artichoke hearts, spinach, and mozzarella cheese, this pizza will be sure to satisfy even the pickiest of eaters.

To prepare this delicious pizza, start by preheating your oven to 375 degrees Fahrenheit. Then unroll the puff pastry sheet onto a greased baking sheet or round stone. Spread the Alfredo sauce over the entire sheet until evenly covered and sprinkle with chopped artichoke hearts, fresh spinach leaves and green onions. Top with sliced mozzarella cheese and shredded parmesan cheese before sprinkling with everything bagel seasoning.

Bake in your preheated oven for 25-30 minutes or until the cheese is golden and bubbly. Let cool slightly before serving and enjoy!

This delicious Spinach Alfredo Pizza is one of many delicious pizza recipes you can make at home and it's sure to be a hit with everyone in the family. Give this delicious pizza recipe a try today and let us know how it turns out! Enjoy!

Spinach And Feta Pizza

Ingredients

2 large Pizza Bases (see notes)
½ cup Tomato Paste.
½ Brown / Yellow Onion, finely diced.
½ Red Capsicum / Bell Pepper, finely diced.
100g / 3.5 oz Baby Spinach, roughly chopped.
4 White Mushrooms, thinly sliced.
½ cup Feta Cheese, crumbled.
1 ½ cups Shredded Mozzarella Cheese (or more, to taste)

Making delicious spinach and feta pizzas is easy and delicious. To begin, preheat your oven to 200°C / 392°F. Place the pizza bases on a lightly greased baking tray. Spread a thin layer of tomato paste over each base, then scatter the diced onion, capsicum / bell pepper, mushrooms, baby spinach and crumbled feta cheese over the top. Sprinkle with mozzarella cheese (you can add more if desired). Bake for 15-20 minutes or until golden brown and bubbly. Serve hot! Enjoy your delicious spinach and feta pizza!

These delicious spinach and feta pizzas are sure to become a family favorite in no time! The combination of flavors from the vegetables, feta and mozzarella cheese makes for a delicious meal that is sure to please everyone. With just a few simple ingredients, you can easily make delicious pizza recipes at home with ease! No need to order take-out anymore - now you can make delicious pizzas right in your own kitchen. Enjoy!

Spinach And Ricotta Pizza

Ingredients

1 batch rustic pizza dough.
1 lb ricotta cheese.
1 lb fontina cheese shredded.
1/4 c parmigiano reggianno grated.
1 1/2 lb garlic spinach.
20 cloves garlic.
pinch of sea salt.
black pepper to taste freshly cracked.

This delicious spinach and ricotta pizza recipe is easy to make and sure to please the whole family. To start, prepare a batch of rustic pizza dough and preheat your oven to 500°F. Once the oven is up to temperature, spread out the pizza dough into a large round shape on an oiled baking sheet or pan.

Next, combine the ricotta cheese, fontina cheese, parmigiano reggianno and garlic together in a bowl until fully combined. Spread this mixture evenly over the pizza dough and top with spinach leaves. Finally, sprinkle some sea salt and freshly cracked black pepper over the pizza before transferring it into the oven for 10-12 minutes or until golden brown and crispy on the edges.

Enjoy your delicious spinach and ricotta pizza straight from the oven for a delicious dinner or lunch. With just a few pre-prepared ingredients, you can have restaurant quality pizza at home in no time. Be sure to share this delicious recipe with your friends and family, they'll love it as much as you do! Bon Appetit!

White Pizza

White pizza is a delicious and unique alternative to the traditional red sauce-topped pizzas. This delicious, garlicky white pizza recipe is sure to be a hit! Prepared with the right ingredients, it can make for a delicious lunch or dinner dish.

To prepare this delicious white pizza, you will need: dough for one large pizza, two tablespoons of olive oil, three minced garlic cloves, eight ounces ball fresh mozzarella sliced thinly, 1/3 cup ricotta cheese, 1/2 teaspoon kosher salt, 1/4 teaspoon freshly ground black pepper, 1/8 teaspoon dried oregano , 1/8 teaspoon dried thyme and 1/3 cup freshly grated Pecorino Romano or Parmesan cheese.

Start by preheating your oven to 375°F and lightly greasing a large, rimmed baking sheet. Unroll the pizza dough onto the pan and press it out into an even thickness. Then, brush the olive oil over the surface of the dough and sprinkle with minced garlic cloves. Layer thinly-sliced mozzarella over top of the garlic and drizzle with ricotta cheese. Sprinkle with salt, pepper, oregano and thyme. Finally, top everything off with freshly grated Pecorino Romano or Parmesan cheese.

Place in preheated oven and bake for 15 to 20 minutes until the crust is golden brown and delicious! Serve hot and enjoy!

This delicious white pizza is sure to be a hit with the whole family. With its garlicky flavor and delicious cheese-topped crust, it makes for a delicious lunch or dinner dish. So why not give this delicious recipe a try tonight? You won't regret it!

Pan Pizza

Making delicious pan pizza is easier than you think with the right ingredients. To make your own delicious pan pizza, start by combining 2 1/4 cups of all-purpose flour and 1 teaspoon of kosher salt in a large bowl. Sprinkle in 3/4 teaspoon of active dry yeast, then add 3/4 cup plus 3 tablespoons of lukewarm water and mix until the dough comes together. Knead the dough on a lightly floured surface for about 5 minutes until it is smooth and elastic. Transfer the dough to an oiled bowl, cover with plastic wrap, and let rise for at least one hour.

Meanwhile, prepare the toppings by mashing two cloves of garlic with one tablespoon olive oil until it forms a paste. Spread one tablespoon of olive oil over the bottom of a greased 10-inch skillet, then roll out the dough in the pan until it covers the base. Spread the garlic paste and tomato sauce over the dough, sprinkle with some dried oregano, and bake for 18 to 20 minutes at 400°F. Enjoy your delicious pizza hot from the oven!

Making delicious pan pizza does not have to be complicated - all you need is some simple ingredients and a few steps to get started. With just a little patience and practice, you can create delicious pizzas that will impress anyone! Try experimenting with different toppings or flavor combinations to make new delicious recipes each time. So what are you waiting for? Get making delicious pizza in no time!

Happy cooking!

Basil Pizza

Ingredients

1 recipe Pizza Dough, stretched onto a 14-inch pizza
pan or large baking sheet.
½ heaping cup Pizza Sauce.
8 ounces fresh mozzarella cheese, torn or sliced.
½ cup thinly sliced cherry tomatoes.
10 fresh basil leaves.
Pinch red pepper flakes.
Extra-virgin olive oil, for drizzling.

This delicious homemade basil pizza is sure to be a hit with your family and friends. Start by preheating the oven to 450°F (232°C). Then, stretch out one recipe of Pizza Dough onto a 14-inch pizza pan or large baking sheet. Spread ½ heaping cup of Pizza Sauce over the dough, followed by 8 ounces of torn or sliced fresh mozzarella cheese, ½ cup thinly sliced cherry tomatoes, 10 fresh basil leaves, and a pinch of red pepper flakes. Drizzle lightly with extra-virgin olive oil before baking in the preheated oven for 17-20 minutes until golden brown. Serve hot as an appetizer or main course! This delicious basil pizza recipe is sure to become one of your go-to delicious pizza recipes. Enjoy!

Veggie Pizza

If you're looking to make delicious veggie pizza, here's a delicious recipe that will get the job done. Start by preheating your oven to 425°F and preparing your ingredients. You'll need store-bought or homemade pizza sauce, vegan mozzarella cheese (optional), sliced red and green bell peppers, onions (white or yellow), mushrooms of your choice, olives (sliced black are traditional but other varieties like kalamata or castelvetrano can be delicious!), dried oregano, and fresh basil.

Instructions for assembling your pizza: spread the pizza sauce over a prepared crust and top with the cheese and veggies. Sprinkle with oregano before baking for 15-20 minutes or until the cheese is melted and the crust is golden. Finally, garnish with fresh basil before slicing and serving. Enjoy!

Creating delicious veggie pizza doesn't have to be complicated or time-consuming. With this simple recipe, you can make a delicious meal in no time. Whether it's for lunch, dinner, or a snack, you can rest assured that your pizza will be delicious every time! Bon appetit!

Goat Cheese Pizza

Goat Cheese Pizza is a delicious recipe that is both easy to make and delicious to eat. This delicious pizza combines delicious ingredients like homemade pizza sauce, mozzarella cheese, soft goat cheese, red onion slices and oregano into a delicious combination that will have your family coming back for seconds!

To start off this delicious meal, you will need one recipe of either the Best Pizza Dough, Thin Crust Pizza Dough or Pizza Oven Dough. Once you have the dough prepared, spread ⅓ cup of Homemade Pizza Sauce on top. Then sprinkle ½ cup of shredded mozzarella cheese over top. Break up 3 ounces of soft goat cheese (chevre) and dot it around the pizza. Lastly add 1 handful of red onion slices and a sprinkle of ¼ teaspoon dried oregano. Finish off the pizza by adding some kosher salt and fresh ground black pepper to taste.

Once all your delicious ingredients are added, bake in an oven preheated to 500°F for 10-15 minutes or until the cheese is melted and bubbly. For a delicious finishing touch, garnish with some fresh basil leaves before serving.

Try this delicious Goat Cheese Pizza recipe tonight and enjoy delicious, easy-to-make pizza that's sure to be a hit! Enjoy!

Focaccia Pizza

If you're looking for delicious pizza recipes, then look no further than focaccia pizza! This popular Italian dish is simple to prepare and full of delicious tastes. To get started, you'll need the following ingredients: 3 cups (15oz/422g) all-purpose flour, ½ teaspoon instant yeast, 2 teaspoons salt, 1 ⅓ cups (10 ½oz/282ml) water at room temperature, 2 tablespoons olive oil, ½ cup (4oz/115g) pizza sauce, 1 ½ cups (8oz/225g) mozzarella grated, and 10-12 pepperoni slices (optional).

To begin preparing this delicious dish, preheat your oven to 450°F. In a large bowl, mix together the flour, yeast, and salt. Once that's done, add in the water and olive oil and stir until a dough is formed. Knead it for 5 minutes on a lightly floured surface. Grease a 14-inch baking pan with olive oil before transferring your dough to it. Press the dough into the pan using your fingertips to form an even layer. Brush with additional oil if needed, then bake at 450°F for 12 minutes.

Once the crust has cooked through, remove from oven and spread pizza sauce over top followed by mozzarella and pepperoni (if desired). Bake again for 10-15 minutes or until cheese is melted and bubbling. Let cool slightly before cutting into slices and serving. Enjoy your delicious focaccia pizza!

You can also customize this delicious dish by adding any additional toppings of your choice! From mushrooms to bell peppers, the possibilities are endless. Give it a try and let us know how delicious your focaccia pizza turned out! Bon Appétit!

Cheese Shrimp Pizza

If you are looking for a delicious pizza recipe with shrimp, this is it! This delicious pizza combines the cheesy goodness of Gruyere and mozzarella cheeses along with delicious shrimp for an unbeatable combination. The dough is prepared and topped with a generous drizzle of olive oil before adding on the cheese, garlic, lemon zest, and parmesan cheese. Once cooked through in the oven, this delicious shrimp pizza will be ready to devour!

To prepare this delicious pizza, start by preheating your oven to 400°F while you prepare the dough. Roll out the dough into a 12-inch circle or rectangle if desired and place onto a greased baking sheet. Drizzle some of the olive oil onto the dough before topping with the Gruyere and mozzarella cheese. In a medium bowl, combine the shrimp, garlic, lemon zest and remaining olive oil. Mix together until completely combined then spread evenly onto the pizza dough. Sprinkle with parmesan cheese and bake in preheated oven for 25 minutes or until crust is golden brown and shrimp is cooked through.

Enjoy this delicious pizza recipe! The combination of cheeses, garlic, lemon zest, shrimp and parmesan cheese makes it irresistible! Enjoy your delicious shrimp pizza!

Pesto Pizza

Are you looking for delicious pizza recipes? Making a pesto pizza is one of the best ways to enjoy a delicious and unique meal. With just a few simple ingredients, you can make this delicious homemade pizza in no time. Here's how to prepare it:

To start, preheat your oven to 425°F (220°C). Spread some cornmeal on your work surface and roll out the dough into desired size. Place the dough onto a baking sheet lined with parchment paper or lightly greased with olive oil.

Spread basil pesto over the dough using ½ cup of olive oil. Top with mozzarella cheese and roasted cherry tomatoes or sun-dried tomatoes. Bake in preheated oven until golden brown and bubbly, 18 to 20 minutes.

Once cooked, top with fresh basil and red pepper flakes for added flavor. Enjoy your delicious pesto pizza! It's a great addition to any meal or served as an appetizer. Bon appétit!

Pickle Pizza

Ingredients

1 recipe pizza dough (or store bought)
2 Tablespoons olive oil.
1 cup garlic pizza sauce.
4 cups shredded mozzarella cheese.
16 oz dill pickle slices, drained and patted dry.
dried or fresh dill, for garnish.

Pickle pizza is one of the delicious pizza recipes you can prepare at home. To make pickle pizza, start by preheating your oven to 400°F (204°C). Then, roll out the pizza dough on a greased baking sheet and brush it with olive oil. Spread the garlic pizza sauce over the dough and top it with shredded mozzarella cheese and dill pickle slices. Bake in preheated oven for 20 minutes or until golden brown. Sprinkle fresh or dried dill over the top before serving for extra flavor! Enjoy this unique and delicious twist on classic pizza!

Pickle pizza is sure to be a delicious hit with family and friends! With just a few simple ingredients, you can make an delicious homemade pickle pizza that everyone will love. Try this delicious recipe today and enjoy the unique flavor of pickles and cheese on your next pizza night!

Breakfast Pizza

1 pound ground breakfast sausage. Great Value
Premium Original Ground Breakfast Sausage, 1 lb.
1 (8 ounce) package refrigerated crescent rolls.
1 cup frozen hash brown potatoes, thawed.
1 cup shredded Cheddar cheese.
5 eggs.
¼ cup milk.
½ teaspoon salt.
⅛ teaspoon ground black pepper.

This delicious pizza recipe is sure to become a favorite for breakfast! It's easy to prepare and all you need are a few simple ingredients. To make this delicious breakfast pizza, begin by preheating the oven to 375°F.

Next, in a large skillet over medium-high heat, cook the sausage until it is cooked through and beginning to brown. Drain off any excess fat from the cooked sausage before transferring it to an ungreased 12-inch pizza pan. Press the crescent roll dough onto the bottom of the pan and spread it out evenly with your fingertips or a spoon. Sprinkle on top of the sausage layer then spread out the hash brown potatoes evenly as well.

In a separate bowl, whisk together the eggs, milk, salt and pepper. Pour this mixture over the pizza ingredients in the pan and top with the shredded cheese. Bake for 25 minutes until golden brown. Let it cool slightly before serving.

With delicious sausage, hash browns and cheddar cheese, this breakfast pizza is sure to become a favorite! Enjoy it warm and savor this delicious recipe any time of day! This is definitely one of our go-to delicious pizza recipes. Have fun trying it out!

Anchovy Pizza

INGREDIENTS

1 BALL BEST PIZZA DOUGH (OR FOOD PROCESSOR
DOUGH OR THIN CRUST DOUGH)
⅓ CUP BEST HOMEMADE PIZZA SAUCE
2 TO 3 OUNCES FRESH MOZZARELLA CHEESE
6 ANCHOVY FILLETS FROM A JAR OR CAN
8 KALAMATA OLIVES
1 HANDFUL THINLY SLICED RED ONION
PARMESAN OR PECORINO CHEESE, FOR GRATING
SEMOLINA FLOUR OR CORNMEAL, FOR DUSTING THE
PIZZA PEEL

Do you love delicious pizza recipes? Try this anchovy pizza for a delicious meal your family and friends will love. It is easy to prepare and takes about 45 minutes from start to finish!

To make this delicious pizza, begin by preheating the oven to 500°F (260°C). Take the Best Pizza Dough (or Food Processor Dough or Thin Crust Dough) and stretch it into a 12-inch circle on a lightly floured surface. Place the dough onto a pizza peel that has been dusted with semolina flour or cornmeal. Spread the Best Homemade Pizza Sauce across the top of the dough, leaving a ½-inch border around the edge. Top with sliced mozzarella cheese, anchovy fillets, Kalamata olives, and red onion.

Move the pizza onto a preheated baking stone or baking sheet in the oven. Bake for 8 to 10 minutes, until the crust is crisp and golden brown. Remove from the oven and top with freshly grated Parmesan or Pecorino cheese. Slice and serve your delicious anchovy pizza right away! Enjoy!

Mexican Pizza

Ingredients

ground beef.
packet of taco seasoning (or homemade)
water.
oil.
corn tortillas.
refried beans.
red enchilada sauce.
shredded cheddar cheese.

Mexican Pizza is one of the delicious pizza recipes you can prepare in no time. It's a delicious, cheesy, and flavorful dish that everyone will love. Plus, it's so easy to make! Here's how to make Mexican Pizza:

1. Start by browning ground beef in a skillet over medium-high heat with some oil. Once cooked through, add taco seasoning mix and water according to package instructions and simmer for 5 minutes until thickened.

2. Spray or lightly brush both sides of corn tortillas with oil and place on baking sheet. Bake at 350 degrees for 10 minutes ("crisp up" the tortillas).

3. Spread refried beans over the "crisped up" tortillas. Top with cooked ground beef and sprinkle with shredded cheddar cheese.

4. Bake in preheated oven at 350 degrees for 15 minutes or until cheese is melted and bubbly.

5. Finally, top the Mexican Pizza with red enchilada sauce (or salsa) and any additional toppings of your choice such as onions, tomatoes, olives, jalapenos, etc. Serve immediately while hot! Enjoy!

Ricotta Pizza

If you're looking for delicious pizza recipes that won't take too long to prepare, look no further than ricotta pizza! This delicious meal combines the delicious flavors of ricotta cheese, mozzarella cheese, Parmesan cheese and artichoke hearts in a delicious combination. To make this delicious pizza, you'll need one ball of Best Pizza Dough (or Thin Crust Dough), ½ cup whole milk ricotta cheese, ⅛ teaspoon kosher salt to taste, fresh ground black pepper, ½ small garlic clove (¼ teaspoon minced), ½ cup shredded mozzarella cheese and ¼ cup shredded Parmesan cheese.

To begin the recipe, preheat your oven to 400°F. Roll out the dough into a 12-inch round and place on a baking sheet. Spread the ricotta cheese over the dough in an even layer, then sprinkle with salt and pepper to taste. Sprinkle the minced garlic, mozzarella cheese and artichoke hearts over the top of the pizza. Finally, sprinkle with Parmesan cheese and bake for 20-25 minutes or until golden brown. Enjoy!

This delicious ricotta pizza is sure to become a favorite in your house! It's quick and easy to prepare, yet delicious enough that everyone will enjoy it. Serve this delicious meal for dinner or as an appetizer at your next gathering—it won't disappoint!

Truffle Pizza

Truffle pizza is a delicious and unique way to enjoy pizza. To make this delicious pizza recipe, you'll need the following ingredients: 1 ball of Best Pizza Dough (or Food Processor Dough or Thin Crust Dough), 6 baby bella mushrooms (aka cremini), 1 garlic clove, 1 handful of chives, 1 tablespoon of olive oil plus more for drizzling, ¾ cup of shredded mozzarella cheese, and ¼ cup Parmesan cheese. In addition, you will need semolina flour or cornmeal to dust your pizza peel.

To prepare the truffle pizza first preheat oven to 425 degrees F. Roll out the dough on a lightly floured surface into desired shape. Place rolled-out dough onto a pizza peel or cookie sheet dusted with semolina flour or cornmeal.

Next, finely chop the mushrooms and garlic clove and add to a bowl with chives and olive oil. Mix together well. Spread this mixture evenly onto your prepared pizza dough, top with mozzarella cheese and Parmesan cheese. Place the pizza in preheated oven for about 8 minutes or until the crust is golden brown. Remove from oven, let cool slightly before slicing into desired pieces. Enjoy!

This delicious truffle pizza recipe is sure to be a hit with your family and friends! With just a few simple ingredients you can create an amazing delicious meal that everyone will love. Try this delicious truffle

Mushroom Pizza

Ingredients

2 tablespoons olive oil.
2 tablespoons unsalted butter.
3 cloves garlic, minced.
16 ounces cremini mushrooms, thinly sliced.
½ teaspoon dried thyme.
½ teaspoon dried oregano.
Kosher salt and freshly ground black pepper, to taste.
¼ cup yellow cornmeal.

For delicious pizza recipes, this mushroom pizza is a must-try. To prepare it, start by preheating the oven to 375 degrees F (190 degrees C). Then heat the olive oil and butter in a large skillet over medium heat. Add garlic and mushrooms and cook until they are softened, about 5 minutes. Stir in thyme, oregano, salt and pepper.
Next, sprinkle some cornmeal onto a baking sheet or pizza pan. Spread the mushroom mixture evenly over the dough then bake for about 15 minutes or until the crust is lightly browned and crispy.
Serve your delicious mushroom pizza warm with your favorite toppings like cheese or fresh herbs!

Mediterranean Pizza

Mediterranean pizza is a delicious and healthy way to enjoy pizza night. It's packed full of vegetables and delicious flavors that will leave you wanting more. The key to making the perfect Mediterranean pizza is picking the right ingredients. Here are some delicious options to try when making your own Mediterranean pizza:

- Hummus: This creamy dip gives an incredible flavor boost to any vegetarian dish, including pizzas. Spread hummus across the base of your pie before adding other toppings for a delicious twist on traditional tomato sauce.
- Green And Red Peppers: Bell peppers have an amazing crunchy texture that pairs perfectly with a cheese-filled crust or even under melted mozzarella cheese. For added color, contrast, and flavor, consider adding both green and red peppers to your Mediterranean pizza.
- Mushrooms: These delicious fungi are a great source of protein and, when cooked correctly, provide an earthy flavor that can't be beaten. Try adding mushrooms with some white cheese for an unbeatable combination.
- Zucchini: For added crunch and flavor, try grilling or sautéing zucchini before adding it to your pizza. The delicious veggie pairs perfectly with pesto, goat cheese, and other delicious flavors found in Mediterranean pizzas.
- Sun-Dried Tomatoes: These intensely flavored tomatoes add a sweet touch to any dish they are put into - including pizza! They go amazingly well with pesto and are a delicious addition to any Mediterranean pizza.

- Pesto: Pesto is a delicious Italian sauce that can be used as the base of any vegetarian dish, including pizzas. Add it with some mushrooms, zucchini, and sun-dried tomatoes for an unbeatable combination.
- Goat Cheese: This delicious cheese has a strong flavor that pairs perfectly with all the delicious ingredients found on Mediterranean pizzas. Try adding crumbled goat cheese over the top for added flavor.

When making your own Mediterranean pizza at home, there's no limit to what you can add or how delicious it can be! Feel free to experiment with different combinations of veggies, sauces and cheeses until you find your perfect pizza. Enjoy!

Egg Pizza

Egg pizza is a delicious, easy to make snack that everyone can enjoy. It's full of flavor and the perfect treat for any occasion. To prepare egg pizza, you will need the following ingredients: 4 eggs, 1 medium onion, 3 thinly sliced cherry tomatoes, 1/2 cup finely chopped capsicum (green pepper), black pepper as required, 2 thinly sliced mushrooms, 1/2 cup grated cheese-cheddar and 1 tablespoon of refined oil.

First begin by preheating your oven to 375 degrees Fahrenheit. Then heat one tablespoon of oil in a pan over medium heat and add the onions. Cook until they start turning golden brown and then add the capsicum and mushroom slices. Cook for a few minutes and then add the eggs. Use a spatula to break the eggs and stir occasionally until they are cooked through and there is no visible liquid egg yolk.

Next, spread the mixture onto a greased baking pan. Top with thinly sliced cherry tomatoes, black pepper and grated cheese-cheddar. Bake in preheated oven for 15 minutes or until the cheese has melted and the pizza is lightly browned. Let it cool slightly before cutting into slices and serve hot with your favorite dip! Enjoy delicious Egg Pizza anytime you want!

This delicious recipe makes an excellent snack or light meal that can be easily prepared at home. With this simple guide, you will have delicious Egg Pizza in no time! Try out this delicious pizza recipe today and create delicious memories with your loved ones. Bon Appetit!

Diavola Pizza

Diavola pizza is a delicious Italian dish that will tantalize your taste buds and make you come back for more. This delicious pizza recipe is made with Best Pizza Dough, Easy Pizza Sauce, fresh mozzarella cheese, Kalamata olives, Fresno or Calabrian chili pepper, and basil leaves. It's simple to prepare and can be ready in no time!

To begin making the diavola pizza, start by rolling out your chosen dough on a lightly floured surface into a 12-inch circle. Place the dough onto an oiled baking sheet or pizza stone. Spread ⅓ cup of homemade easy pizza sauce over the dough evenly leaving one inch around the edges. Top with 4 ounces of fresh mozzarella cheese and a sprinkle of kosher salt if desired. Add 8 to 10 Kalamata olives, one Fresno or Calabrian chili pepper, and two basil leaves to the top of the pizza.

Once all your delicious toppings are in place, bake at 475°F for about 18 minutes until the crust is golden brown and the cheese has melted and bubbled. Let cool for five minutes before serving warm. Enjoy!

Now that you have the recipe for this delicious diavola pizza, why not give it a try? The combination of flavors is sure to make this dish a favorite in your household. Serve with a delicious side salad or some garlic bread to complete the meal! Enjoy

Neapolitan Pizza

Ingredients

1 ball Best Homemade Pizza Dough.
⅓ cup Easy Pizza Sauce.
3 ounces fresh mozzarella cheese (or
about ¾ cup shredded mozzarella)
Kosher salt.
2 basil leaves.
Semolina flour or cornmeal, for
dusting the pizza peel.

Making delicious neapolitan pizza at home is easier than you think! All you need are a few simple ingredients and the right technique.

Start by preheating your oven to 500°F or higher. Place a pizza stone in the oven to heat up, as well. Next, prepare the dough. Roll out 1 ball of Best Homemade Pizza Dough on a lightly floured surface until it's about 10 inches in diameter. Transfer the dough onto a pizza peel dusted with semolina flour or cornmeal.
Spread ⅓ cup of Easy Pizza Sauce over the top of your crust and sprinkle with kosher salt. Add 3 ounces (or ¾ cup) of fresh mozzarella cheese and 2 basil leaves. Carefully slide the pizza off the peel onto the preheated pizza stone in the oven and bake for 8 to 10 minutes until golden brown.
Enjoy your delicious homemade neapolitan pizza! For more delicious pizza recipes, you can check out our website or visit us on social media. We look forward to hearing how you prepared this delicious meal! Bon Appétit!

Tuna Pizza

Ingredients

1 (8 ounce) package cream cheese, softened.
1 (14 ounce) package pre-baked pizza crust.
1 (5 ounce) can tuna, drained and flaked.
½ cup thinly sliced red onion.
1 ½ cups shredded mozzarella cheese.
crushed red pepper flakes, or to taste.

Tuna pizza is a delicious, easy-to-make recipe that will satisfy both seafood lovers and pizza enthusiasts. This delicious combination of cream cheese, tuna, red onion, and mozzarella cheese is sure to become one of your favorite delicious pizza recipes! To prepare this delicious treat, follow the steps below:

Firstly, preheat your oven to 375°F (190°C). Next, spread the softened cream cheese on the pre-baked pizza crust. Then add the flaked tuna, red onion slices, and shredded mozzarella cheese on top. Sprinkle some crushed red pepper flakes over the top according to taste. Finally, bake in preheated oven for 15 minutes or until cheese has melted and edges of crust are golden brown.

Enjoy your delicious tuna pizza! If you're looking for more delicious pizza recipes, be sure to check out our other delicious pizza recipes.
Bon Appetit!

Buffalo Chicken Pizza

Ingredients

1 tube (13.8 ounces) refrigerated pizza crust.
1 cup Buffalo wing sauce, divided.
1-1/2 cups shredded cheddar cheese.
1-1/2 cups part-skim shredded mozzarella cheese.
2 pounds boneless skinless chicken breasts, cubed.
1/2 teaspoon each garlic salt, pepper and chili powder.
2 tablespoons butter.

This delicious buffalo chicken pizza recipe is the perfect way to bring together the spicy and tangy flavors of Buffalo wing sauce with delicious cheese and tender chunks of chicken. Start by unrolling the refrigerated pizza crust onto a greased baking sheet. Brush half of the Buffalo wing sauce over crust before adding a layer of cheeses, followed by cubed chicken that has been seasoned with garlic salt, pepper and chili powder. Finally, brush remaining wing sauce over top before baking for 12-15 minutes in an oven preheated to 425°F. Enjoy this delicious buffalo chicken pizza as is or serve with ranch dressing for extra deliciousness! The result will be a delicious, cheesy and spicy meal everyone will love! So why not give it a try and enjoy delicious pizza recipes at home? You won't be disappointed!

This buffalo chicken pizza is easy to prepare and the delicious result will make you glad you tried it. All you need to do is start by unrolling the refrigerated pizza crust onto a greased baking sheet, brush half of the Buffalo wing sauce over crust before adding a layer of cheeses, followed by cubed chicken that has been seasoned with garlic salt, pepper and chili powder. Finally, brush remaining wing sauce over top before baking for 12-15 minutes in an oven preheated to 425°F. Enjoy your delicious homemade buffalo chicken pizza served hot or cold! It's sure to become a family favorite.

Bacon Chicken Pizza

Making delicious pizza recipes at home is easier than you think! This bacon chicken pizza is packed with delicious flavors and takes only minutes to prepare. To get started, gather the following ingredients: 60g of shortcut bacon, sliced; 200g of wholemeal Lebanese bread; 125g tomato passata; 150g button mushrooms, thinly sliced; 1/2 medium red capsicum, thinly sliced; 1/2 medium red onion, thinly sliced; 200g cooked skinless chicken breast, shredded; and 1 cup reduced-fat mozzarella cheese, shredded.

To begin preparation for your delicious pizza recipe, preheat your oven to 220°C (200°C fan). Place the Lebanese bread on a baking tray lined with baking paper. Spread the tomato passata evenly over the bread, followed by the mushrooms, red capsicum and onion. Then top with the bacon and chicken. Finally, scatter the cheese over the pizza and bake for 20 minutes or until golden brown.

Your delicious bacon chicken pizza is now ready to be enjoyed! Serve hot or cold, it's guaranteed to make an impression on your guests this summer! Enjoy!

Seafood Pizza

Seafood pizza is a delicious and unique dish that will tantalize your taste buds with its delicious combination of flavors. This delicious pizza recipe starts off with 12 uncooked medium fresh shrimp, which are kept in their shells for added flavor. The base of this delicious seafood pizza is 1 cup of pizza sauce, followed by 1 cup of shredded mozzarella cheese (4 oz) and 1/2 cup of shredded provolone cheese (2 oz). To give the pizza an extra boost of flavor, 8 anchovy fillets in oil and 1/2 lb bay scallops are added. Finally, the dish is topped with a sprinkle of 1/2 cup chopped fresh basil leaves and 1/2 teaspoon pepper to enhance the flavor even further.

This delicious pizza recipe is easy to follow and can be prepared in just a few steps. First, preheat your oven to 375°F and prepare a baking sheet with parchment paper or foil. Place the shrimp on the sheet and bake for about 8-10 minutes until cooked through. Once the shrimp are done cooking, remove them from the oven and let cool before preparing the rest of the pizza. Spread the pizza sauce over a pre-made or pre-bought crust, then sprinkle with both cheeses followed by anchovies, scallops, basil leaves, pepper, and finally cooked shrimp. Bake this delicious seafood pizza at 375°F for 12-15 minutes until golden brown. Enjoy!

For delicious pizza recipes that are sure to please, try out this delicious seafood pizza. With its combination of delicious ingredients and easy preparation steps, you'll be able to enjoy a delicious meal in no time!

Tomato Baguette Pizza

Ingredients

8 ounces sliced fresh mushrooms.
2 medium onions, halved and sliced.
2 garlic cloves, minced.
3/4 cup thinly sliced fresh basil leaves, divided.
3 medium tomatoes, sliced.
1/2 teaspoon Italian seasoning.
2 teaspoons olive oil.
1 French bread baguette (10-1/2 ounces),
halved lengthwise.

This delicious pizza recipe is a great way to use up fresh tomatoes and baguettes. To prepare the pizza, preheat your oven to 375°F. In a large skillet, sauté mushrooms, onions, and garlic in olive oil until tender-crisp. Add 1/2 cup of basil leaves and Italian seasoning; cook for one minute more. Spread tomato slices over the cut sides of the baguette halves and top with mushroom mixture. Sprinkle remaining 1/4 cup of basil leaves over each half. Bake for 15 minutes or until heated through. Serve warm and enjoy! With this delicious pizza recipe, you can bring delicious flavors into your kitchen without having to leave home! Enjoy!

Turkey Alfredo Pizza

Turkey Alfredo Pizza is a delicious Italian-style pizza that combines turkey, spinach, and creamy Alfredo sauce for an unforgettable meal. This delicious pizza recipe is incredibly easy to prepare and can be whipped up in no time.

To begin preparing this delicious pizza, preheat the oven to 425 degrees Fahrenheit. Place a prebaked 12-inch thin pizza crust on a baking sheet and set aside. Next, rub the cut side of a garlic clove onto the crust and spread ½ cup of reduced-fat Alfredo sauce over it.

In a medium bowl, combine thawed and squeezed dry frozen chopped spinach with lemon juice. Spread the mixture evenly over the prepared crust and sprinkle 2 cups of shredded cooked turkey breast over the spinach. Drizzle the remaining ¼ cup of Alfredo sauce over the turkey and top with 3/4 cup of shredded Parmesan cheese.

Place in preheated oven and bake for 15-18 minutes, or until pizza crust is golden brown and cheese is melted. Cut into slices and serve hot. Enjoy!

With just a few simple ingredients, you can now make delicious Turkey Alfredo Pizza right in your own home! Not only is this recipe delicious, it's easy to make and full of delicious flavors that will tantalize your taste buds. Try making this delicious pizza today and see how much your family loves it!

Thank you
We hope you enjoyed our book.

As a small family company ,your feedback is very important to us.

Please let us know how you like your book